MODERN *Baby*

LEISURE ARTS, INC. • Maumelle, Arkansas

Knitting has been around for centuries. Its origins, as well as its early years, were marked by knitting as a necessity to clothe and protect from the elements. What was once an essential skill to be passed down from generation to generation has slowly evolved into a hobby that can not only be passed down to future generations, but can be shared with the entire world.

With the growth of the internet, knitters have come together to share patterns, ideas, new techniques and raise awareness of the myriad designs that can be created with a few simple tools – from socks and mittens, to afghans and sweaters, and everything in between.

Included in this book are six varied modern onesie designs that incorporate some of the many techniques now available to knitters.

> The projects are small enough to finish quickly while learning a new skill.

Starting with a simpler stockinette version on page 48, consumers can learn short row techniques and raglan shaping. Once that is mastered, they can move on to more challenging techniques, such as twisted stitches, seed stitch motifs, lace, and cables. The projects are small enough to finish quickly while learning a new skill.

The onesies and matching hats make perfect gifts for those precious little bundles of joy. Knitted all in one piece, there are no seams to sew. Worsted weight yarn was used in creating these designs to not only make a quick and delightful project, but to capitalize on the bountiful variety of yarns and colors available on the market. They might also be the perfect project to use up stash yarn leftover from other projects. Once you make one, the other designs will be calling out to you!

Judy Lamb

Sweaters, both big and small, are Judy Lamb's favorite knitting projects, along with scarves, hats, and gloves.

"My grandmother taught me to knit at the age of 8," she says, "but it wasn't until my college years that I was bitten by the knitting bug. My first project was a complete disaster, but it taught me some very important lessons in the craft of knitting, such as gauge, and that not all yarn is the same. Undaunted, I dove in to learn all I could about the craft, and my next project — a baby sweater that my first child proudly wore — converted me completely." Judy now loves to shower her grandchildren with her creations.

> "My first project was a complete disaster, but it taught me some very important lessons in the craft of knitting, such as gauge, and that not all yarn is the same."

"I think what inspires me the most is the fascination that so many beautiful things can be made with a couple of sticks and a long string. Creating something that is uniquely my own design, and to see it actually turn into a finished product, is what drives me."

Judy also enjoys playing the piano, cooking, reading, writing, sewing, crocheting, tatting, and dabbling in bobbin lacework. For more of her designs, visit LeisureArts.com and jaslamb.weebly.com.

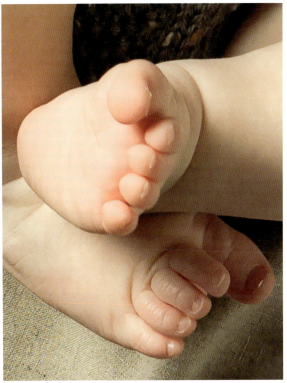

contents

ALL-OF-A-TWIST	8
BABY LOVE	16
DIAMOND BROCADE	24
FRAMED CABLE	32
LACE ACCENT	40
MIXED BERRY	48
GENERAL INSTRUCTIONS	56
YARN INFORMATION	63

ALL-OF-A-TWIST

●●●○ **INTERMEDIATE**

SHOPPING LIST

Yarn (Medium Weight) 🧶4
[5 ounces, 256 yards
(141 grams, 234 meters) per skein]:
☐ 2 skeins

Knitting Needles
Double-pointed (set of 5),
☐ Size 6 (4 mm) **and**
☐ Size 8 (5 mm)
or sizes needed for gauge
Straight,
☐ Size 8 (5 mm) (for Leg Bands)

Note: A 36" (91.5 cm) circular needle may be used for the Magic Loop Method

Additional Supplies
☐ Split-ring marker
☐ Stitch markers
☐ Scrap yarn (to use as st holders)
☐ Yarn needle
☐ ⅝" (15 mm) Buttons - 3
☐ Sewing needle & matching thread

SIZE INFORMATION

Finished Chest Circumference:
{15½-16½}{18¼-18¼-20}"/
{39.5-42}{46.5-46.5-51} cm

Finished Head Circumference:
{14¼-15}{16½-17-17¼}"/
{36-38}{42-43-44} cm

Size Note: We have printed the instructions for the sizes in different colors to make it easier for you to find.

- 0-3 months in Blue
- 3-6 months in Pink
- 6-9 months in Green
- 9-12 months in Red
- 12-18 months in Purple

Instructions in Black apply to all sizes.

GAUGE INFORMATION
With larger size needles,
in Stockinette Stitch
(knit every round),
18 sts and 24 rnds = 4" (10 cm)

STITCH GUIDE
DOUBLE INCREASE (uses one st)
(K, YO, K) **all** in the st indicated.
RIGHT TWIST (abbreviated RT)
(uses next 2 sts)
K2 tog but do not slip sts from left needle, knit the first st again letting both sts off of left needle.

TECHNIQUES USED
- YO *(Fig. 3a, page 58)*
- kfb *(Figs. 4a & b, page 59)*
- K2 tog *(Fig. 5, page 59)*
- P2 tog *(Fig. 6, page 59)*
- SSK *(Figs. 7a-c, page 59)*

ONESIE

IMPORTANT! In order for the baby's head to fit through the neck opening, your stitches must be cast on with two larger size needles held together. Then slide the extra needle out and divide the stitches evenly onto four smaller double-pointed needles, or in half for the Magic Loop Method.

Onesie is worked in one piece from the Neck down.

Yoke
NECK RIBBING
Cast on {44-48}{52-56-60} sts. Slip one-fourth of the sts onto **each** of 4 smaller size double-pointed needles *(see Double-Pointed Needles, page 57)*; place a split-ring marker to indicate the beginning of the round *(see Markers, page 57)*.

Rnds 1-4: (K1, P1) around.

SHORT ROW SHAPING
Change to larger size needles.

Foundation Rnd: Knit around to last {4-4}{4-5-5} sts, place st marker, remove split-ring marker.

Row 1: Continuing to work in the same direction, double increase in next st, knit {6-6}{6-8-8} sts, double increase in next st, knit {14-16}{18-18-20} sts, double increase in next st, knit {6-6}{6-8-8} sts, double increase in next st, K1, place st marker, wrap & turn *(Fig. 10a, page 61)*.

Row 2: Purl across to next marker, remove st marker, P1, replace st marker, wrap & turn *(Fig. 10b, page 61)*.

Row 3: K2, double increase in next st, knit {8-8}{8-10-10} sts, double increase in next st, knit {16-18}{20-20-22} sts, double increase in next st, knit {8-8}{8-10-10} sts, double increase in next st, K2, remove st marker, knit next st **and** wrap together *(Fig. 10c, page 61)*, replace st marker, wrap & turn.

Row 4: Purl across to next st marker, remove st marker, purl next st **and** wrap together *(Fig. 10d, page 61)*, replace st marker, wrap & turn.

Row 5: K4, double increase in next st, knit {10-10}{10-12-12} sts, double increase in next st, knit {18-20}{22-22-24} sts, double increase in next st, knit {10-10}{10-12-12} sts, double increase in next st, K4, remove st marker, knit next st **and** wrap together, replace st marker, wrap & turn.

Row 6: Purl across to next st marker, remove st marker, purl next st **and** wrap together, replace st marker, wrap & turn.

0-3 months ONLY
Row 7: K6, double increase in next st, K 12, double increase in next st, K 20, double increase in next st, K 12, double increase in next st, K6, slip marker, knit next st **and** wrap together, do **not** turn.

Remaining 4 sizes ONLY
Row 7: K6, double increase in next st, knit {12}{12-14-14} sts, double increase in next st, knit {22}{24-24-26} sts, double increase in next st, knit {12}{12-14-14} sts, double increase in next st, K6, remove st marker, knit next st **and** wrap together, knit {0}{1-1-1} st(s) *(see Zeros, page 58)*, replace st marker, do **not** turn.

SLEEVE SHAPING - ALL SIZES
Foundation Rnd: Knit {6-8}{9-9-11} sts, knit next st **and** wrap together, remove st marker, knit around to next st marker, remove st marker, place split-ring marker around next st (first st of Foundation Rnd) to mark beginning of rnd: {76-80}{84-88-92} sts.

Rnd 1: P2, (kfb, P2) twice, place st marker, knit {7-8}{9-9-10} sts, double increase in next st (center st of previous double increase), knit {14-14}{14-16-16} sts, double increase in next st (center st of previous double increase), knit {22-24}{26-26-28} sts, double increase in next st (center st of previous double increase), knit {14-14}{14-16-16} sts, double increase in next st (center st of previous double increase), knit {7-8}{9-9-10} sts: {86-90}{94-98-102} sts.

Rnd 2: P2, (RT, P2) twice (Rnd 1 of chart on page 12), knit around.

Rnd 3: Work **next** rnd of chart to st marker, knit around working double increase in center st of each previous double increase: {94-98}{102-106-110} sts.

Rnd 4: Work **next** rnd of chart to st marker, knit around.

Repeat Rnds 3 and 4, {2-2} {3-3-4} times; then repeat Rnd 3 once **more**: {118-122}{134-138-150} sts.

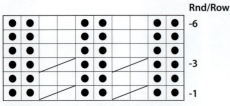

Repeat Rnds/Rows 1-6 for Twist pattern

KEY
☐ knit on RS, purl on WS
● purl on RS, knit on WS
╱ Right Twist

Body

Cut two, 14" (35.5 cm) lengths of scrap yarn to use as st holders.

Dividing Rnd: Work **next** rnd of chart to st marker, ★ knit across to center st of previous double increase, thread yarn needle with scrap yarn and slip the center st, the next {24-24}{26-28-30} sts, and the next center st onto scrap yarn (for Sleeve), cast 3 sts onto right needle using e-wrap method *(Fig. 2, page 58)*, place underarm marker; repeat from ★ once **more**, knit around: {72-76}{84-84-92} sts.

Rnd 1: Work **next** rnd of chart to st marker, knit around.

Repeat Rnd 1 until piece measures approximately {9-10}{11-12-12}"/ {23-25.5}{28-30.5-30.5} cm from top of back neck, ending by working an odd-numbered rnd of chart.

Set-up Rnd: Work **next** rnd of chart to st marker, knit around to second underarm marker, remove marker; bind off next 3 sts, knit across to beginning marker, replace beginning marker with st marker, work **next** rnd of chart to next st marker, knit across to first underarm marker, remove marker; bind off next 3 sts, knit across remaining back sts: {32-34} {38-38-42} Back sts and {34-36} {40-40-44} Front sts.

Back Flap

Leaving Front sts on needle to be worked later, begin working in rows across Back sts.

Row 1 (Decrease row): P2 tog, purl across: {31-33}{37-37-41} sts.

Row 2 (Right side - Decrease row): K2 tog, knit across: {30-32} {36-36-40} sts.

Repeat Rows 1 and 2, {9-10} {12-12-14} times: 12 sts.

Next Row: Purl across.

Decrease Row: K5, K2 tog, K5: 11 sts.

BAND

Rows 1-3: Knit across.

Row 4 (Buttonhole row): K1, YO, K2 tog, (K2, YO, K2 tog) twice: 3 Buttonholes made.

Rows 5-7: Knit across.

Bind of all sts in **knit**.

Front Flap

With **wrong** side facing, attach yarn to beginning of Front sts. Maintain established pattern throughout, working Chart between markers.

Rows 1 and 2: Bind off first {3-3} {3-3-4} sts, work across: {28-30} {34-34-36} sts.

0-3 months, 3-6 months, & 12-18 months ONLY
Rows 3 thru {5-5}{7}: Decrease, work across to last 2 sts, decrease: {22-24} {26} sts.

Row {6-6}{8} (Decrease row): K2 tog, work across to last 2 sts, K2 tog: {20-22}{24} sts.

Row {7-7}{9}: Purl across.

Repeat last 2 rows, {3-4}{5} times: 14 sts.

6-9 months & 9-12 months ONLY
Rows 3-6: Decrease, work across to last 2 sts, decrease: 26 sts.

Row 7: Purl across.

Row 8 (Decrease row): K2 tog, work across to last 2 sts, K2 tog: 24 sts.

Rows 9-19: Repeat Rows 7 and 8, 5 times; then repeat Row 7 once **more** removing markers: 14 sts.

All Sizes
Decrease Row: K2, P2, K2 tog 3 times, P2, K2: 11 sts.

BAND
Rows 1-7: Knit across.

Bind off all sts in **knit**, leave last st on needle; do **not** cut yarn.

Leg Bands
LEFT
Slip remaining st onto straight needles and with **right** side facing, pick up {37-43}{49-53-55} sts along Left leg opening *(Figs. 11a & b, page 61)*: {38-44}{50-54-56} sts.

Rows 1 and 2: Knit across.

Bind off all sts in **knit**.

RIGHT
With **right** side facing and using straight needles, pick up {38-44}{50-54-56} sts along Right leg opening.

Rows 1 and 2: Knit across.

Bind off all sts in **knit**.

Sleeve
With **right** side facing and using larger size needles, pick up {3-3}{5-5-5} sts across cast on edge at underarm, knit across all sts of sleeve, removing scrap yarn and distributing sts evenly on needles to work in the round: {29-29}{33-35-37} sts.

Rnd 1: Knit around.

Repeat Rnd 1 once for Short Sleeve **or** until Sleeve measures approximately {5-5½}{6-6½-7}"/ {12.5-14}{15-16.5-18} cm from underarm for Long Sleeve.

RIBBING

Change to smaller size needles.

Row 1: K1, (P1, K1) around to last 2 sts, P2 tog: {28-28}{32-34-36} sts.

Rows 2 and 3: (K1, P1) around.

Bind off all sts **loosely** in ribbing.

Repeat for second sleeve.

Sew buttons to Front Flap, corresponding to buttonholes on Back Flap.

HAT
Ribbing

With smaller size needles, cast on {64-64}{74-74-74} sts **loosely**.

Slip sts onto 4 double-pointed needles; place a split-ring marker to indicate the beginning of the round.

Rnd 1: (K1, P1) around.

Repeat Rnd 1, 7 times **more** increasing one st on last rnd: {65-65}{75-75-75} sts.

Body

Change to larger size needles.

Foundation Rnd (Right side): ★ P2, kfb, P2, knit {8-8}{10-10-10} sts; repeat from ★ around: {70-70}{80-80-80} sts.

Rnd 1: ★ P2, RT, P2 (Rnd 1 of chart), knit {8-8}{10-10-10} sts; repeat from ★ around.

Rnd 2: ★ Work **next** rnd of chart across next 6 sts, knit {8-8}{10-10-10} sts; repeat from ★ around.

Repeat Rnd 2 until Hat measures approximately {4½-5}{5½-6-6½}"/ {11.5-12.5}{14-15-16.5} cm from cast on edge.

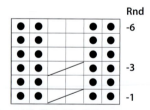

Repeat Rnds 1-6 for Twist pattern

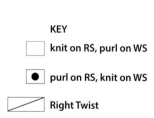

KEY

☐ knit on RS, purl on WS

● purl on RS, knit on WS

╱ Right Twist

SHAPING

Rnd 1: ★ Work **next** rnd of chart across next 6 sts, SSK, knit {4-4}{6-6-6}, K2 tog; repeat from ★ around: {60-60}{70-70-70} sts.

Rnd 2: ★ Work **next** rnd of chart across next 6 sts, knit {6-6}{8-8-8} sts; repeat from ★ around.

Rnd 3: ★ Work **next** rnd of chart across next 6 sts, SSK, knit {2-2}{4-4-4}, K2 tog; repeat from ★ around: {50-50}{60-60-60} sts.

Rnd 4: ★ Work **next** rnd of chart across next 6 sts, knit {4-4}{6-6-6} sts; repeat from ★ around.

Rnd 5: ★ Work **next** rnd of chart across next 6 sts, SSK, knit {0-0}{2-2-2}, K2 tog; repeat from ★ around: {40-40}{50-50-50} sts.

Rnd 6: ★ Work **next** rnd of chart across next 6 sts, knit {2-2}{4-4-4} sts; repeat from ★ around.

6-9 months, 9-12 months, & 12-18 months ONLY

Rnd 7: ★ Work **next** rnd of chart across next 6 sts, SSK, K2 tog; repeat from ★ around: {40-40-40} sts.

Rnd 8: ★ Work **next** rnd of chart across next 6 sts, K2; repeat from ★ around.

All Sizes
K2 tog around until 4 sts remain.

I-CORD
Slip all 4 sts onto one needle so the last st worked is to the left of the other 3 sts. Slide sts to the right end of the needle and K4, ★ do **not** turn, slide sts to opposite end of the needle, K4; repeat from ★ until I-cord measures approximately 3" (7.5 cm).

Cut yarn leaving a 10" (25.5 cm) length for sewing.

Thread yarn needle with long end and slip sts onto yarn needle; gather **tightly** to close and secure end. Tie I-Cord into an overhand knot, tying knot close to Hat.

●●●○ INTERMEDIATE

B-A-B-Y LOVE

SIZE INFORMATION

Finished Chest Circumference:
{15½-16½}{18¼-18¼-20}"/
{39.5-42}{46.5-46.5-51} cm

Finished Head Circumference:
{14¼-15}{16½-17-17¼}"/
{36-38}{42-43-44} cm

Size Note: We have printed the instructions for the sizes in different colors to make it easier for you to find.

- 0-3 months in Blue
- 3-6 months in Pink
- 6-9 months in Green
- 9-12 months in Red
- 12-18 months in Purple

Instructions in Black apply to all sizes.

SHOPPING LIST

Yarn (Medium Weight) [4]
[4 ounces, 203 yards
(113 grams, 186 meters) per skein]:
☐ 2 skeins

Knitting Needles
Double-pointed (set of 5),
☐ Size 6 (4 mm) **and**
☐ Size 8 (5 mm)
or sizes needed for gauge
Straight,
☐ Size 8 (5 mm) (for Leg Bands)

Note: A 36" (91.5 cm) circular needle may be used for the Magic Loop Method

Additional Supplies
☐ Split-ring marker
☐ Stitch markers
☐ Scrap yarn (to use as st holders)
☐ Yarn needle
☐ ¹¹⁄₁₆" (18 mm) Buttons - 3
☐ Purchased pom-pom
☐ Sewing needle & matching thread

GAUGE INFORMATION
With larger size needles,
  in Stockinette Stitch
  (knit every round),
  18 sts and 24 rnds = 4" (10 cm)

STITCH GUIDE
DOUBLE INCREASE (uses one st)
(K, YO, K) **all** in the st indicated.

TECHNIQUES USED
- YO *(Fig. 3a, page 58)*
- K2 tog *(Fig. 5, page 59)*
- P2 tog *(Fig. 6, page 59)*

ONESIE

IMPORTANT! In order for the baby's head to fit through the neck opening, your stitches must be cast on with two larger size needles held together. Then slide the extra needle out and divide the stitches evenly onto four smaller double-pointed needles, or in half for the Magic Loop Method.

Onesie is worked in one piece from the Neck down.

Yoke

NECK RIBBING

Cast on {44-48}{52-56-60} sts. Slip one-fourth of the sts onto **each** of 4 smaller size double-pointed needles *(see Double-Pointed Needles, page 57)*; place a split-ring marker to indicate the beginning of the round *(see Markers, page 57)*.

Rnds 1-4: (K1, P1) around.

SHORT ROW SHAPING

Change to larger size needles.

Foundation Rnd: Knit around to last {4-4}{4-5-5} sts, place st marker, remove split-ring marker.

Row 1: Continuing to work in the same direction, double increase in next st, knit {6-6}{6-8-8} sts, double increase in next st, knit {14-16}{18-18-20} sts, double increase in next st, knit {6-6}{6-8-8} sts, double increase in next st, K1, place st marker, wrap & turn *(Fig. 10a, page 61)*.

Row 2: Purl across to next marker, remove st marker, P1, replace st marker, wrap & turn *(Fig. 10b, page 61)*.

Row 3: K2, double increase in next st, knit {8-8}{8-10-10} sts, double increase in next st, knit {16-18}{20-20-22} sts, double increase in next st, knit {8-8}{8-10-10} sts, double increase in next st, K2, remove st marker, knit next st **and** wrap together *(Fig. 10c, page 61)*, replace st marker, wrap & turn.

Row 4: Purl across to next st marker, remove st marker, purl next st **and** wrap together *(Fig. 10d, page 61)*, replace st marker, wrap & turn.

Row 5: K4, double increase in next st, knit {10-10}{10-12-12} sts, double increase in next st, knit {18-20}{22-22-24} sts, double increase in next st, knit {10-10}{10-12-12} sts,

double increase in next st, K4, remove st marker, knit next st **and** wrap together, replace st marker, wrap & turn.

Row 6: Purl across to next st marker, remove st marker, purl next st **and** wrap together, replace st marker, wrap & turn.

Row 7: K6, double increase in next st, knit {12-12}{12-14-14} sts, double increase in next st, knit {20-22}{24-24-26} sts, double increase in next st, knit {12-12}{12-14-14} sts, double increase in next st, K6, remove st marker, knit next st **and** wrap together, knit {0-1}{2-2-3} sts *(see Zeros, page 58)*, replace st marker, do **not** turn.

SLEEVE SHAPING

Foundation Rnd: Knit {6-7}{8-8-9} sts, knit next st **and** wrap together, remove st marker, knit across to next st marker (remaining marker now indicates the beginning of the rnd): {76-80}{84-88-92} sts.

Rnd 1: Knit {14-15}{16-16-17} sts, double increase in next st, knit {14-14}{14-16-16} sts, double increase in next st, knit {22-24}{26-26-28} sts, double increase in next st, knit {14-14}{14-16-16} sts, double increase in next st, knit {8-9}{10-10-11} sts: {84-88}{92-96-100} sts.

Rnd 2: Knit around.

Rnd 3: Knit {15-16}{17-17-18} sts, double increase in next st (center st of previous double increase), knit {16-16}{16-18-18} sts, double increase in next st (center st of previous double increase), knit {24-26}{28-28-30} sts, double increase in next st (center st of previous double increase), knit {16-16}{16-18-18} sts, double increase in next st (center st of previous double increase), knit {9-10}{11-11-12} sts: {92-96}{100-104-108} sts.

Rnd 4: Knit around.

Rnd 5: P5, K1 (Rnd 1 of Letter B chart on page 20), place st marker, knit around working double increase in center st of each previous double increase: {100-104}{108-112-116} sts.

Rnd 6: Work **next** rnd of chart to marker, knit around.

Rnd 7: Work **next** rnd of chart to marker, knit around working double increase in center st of each previous double increase: {108-112}{116-120-124} sts.

Repeat Rnds 6 and 7, {1-1}{2-2-3} time(s); then repeat Rnd 6 once **more**: {116-120}{132-136-148} sts.

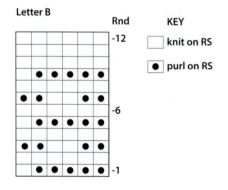

Letter B

Body

Cut two, 14" (35.5 cm) lengths of scrap yarn to use as st holders.

Dividing Rnd: Work **next** rnd of chart to st marker, ★ knit across to center st of previous double increase, thread yarn needle with scrap yarn and slip the center st, the next {24-24}{26-28-30} sts, and the next center st onto scrap yarn (for Sleeve), cast 3 sts onto right needle using e-wrap method *(Fig. 2, page 58)*, place underarm marker; repeat from ★ once **more**, knit around: {70-74}{82-82-90} sts.

Note: After all rounds of the Letter B chart are worked, work all rnds of the Letter A chart, then repeat the Letter B chart, then the Letter Y chart.

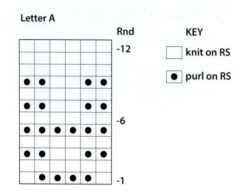

Letter A

Rnd 1: Work **next** rnd of chart to marker, knit around.

Repeat Rnd 1 until all the Letter charts have been worked, then knit every rnd until piece measures approximately {9-10}{11-12-12}"/{23-25.5}{28-30.5-30.5} cm from top of back neck.

Set-up Rnd: Knit around to second underarm marker, remove marker; bind off next 3 sts, knit across to beginning marker, remove marker, knit across to first underarm marker, remove marker; bind off next 3 sts, knit across remaining back sts: {32-34}{38-38-42} Back sts and {32-34}{38-38-42} Front sts.

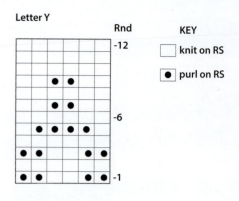

Letter Y

Back Flap

Leaving Front sts on needle to be worked later, begin working in rows across Back sts.

Row 1 (Decrease row): P2 tog, purl across: {31-33}{37-37-41} sts.

Row 2 (Right side - Decrease row): K2 tog, knit across: {30-32}{36-36-40} sts.

Repeat Rows 1 and 2, {9-10}{12-12-14} times: 12 sts.

Next Row: Purl across.

Decrease Row: K5, K2 tog, K5: 11 sts.

BAND

Rows 1-3: Knit across.

Row 4 (Buttonhole row): K1, YO, K2 tog, (K2, YO, K2 tog) twice: 3 Buttonholes made.

Rows 5-7: Knit across.

Bind of all sts in **knit**.

Front Flap

With **wrong** side facing, attach yarn to beginning of Front sts. Maintain established pattern throughout.

Rows 1 and 2: Bind off first {3-3}{3-3-4} sts, work across: {26-28}{32-32-34} sts.

0-3 months, 3-6 months, & 12-18 months ONLY

Rows 3 thru {5-5}{7}: Decrease, work across to last 2 sts, decrease: {20-22}{24} sts.

Row {6-6}{8} (Decrease row): K2 tog, knit across to last 2 sts, K2 tog: {18-20}{22} sts.

Row {7-7}{9}: Purl across.

Repeat last 2 rows, {3-4}{5} times: 12 sts.

6-9 months & 9-12 months ONLY

Rows 3-6: Decrease, work across to last 2 sts, decrease: 24 sts.

Row 7: Purl across.

Row 8 (Decrease row): K2 tog, knit across to last 2 sts, K2 tog: 22 sts.

Rows 9-19: Repeat Rows 7 and 8, 5 times; then repeat Row 7 once **more**: 12 sts.

All Sizes

Decrease Row: K5, K2 tog, K5: 11 sts.

BAND

Rows 1-7: Knit across.

Bind off all sts in **knit**, leave last st on needle; do **not** cut yarn.

Leg Bands

LEFT

Slip remaining st onto straight needles and with **right** side facing, pick up {37-43}{49-53-55} sts along Left leg opening *(Figs. 11a & b, page 61)*: {38-44}{50-54-56} sts.

Rows 1 and 2: Knit across.

Bind off all sts in **knit**.

RIGHT

With **right** side facing and using straight needles, pick up {38-44}{50-54-56} sts along Right leg opening.

Rows 1 and 2: Knit across.

Bind off all sts in **knit**.

Sleeve

With **right** side facing and using larger size needles, pick up {3-3}{5-5-5} sts across cast on edge at underarm, knit across all sts of sleeve, removing scrap yarn and distributing sts evenly on needles to work in the round: {29-29}{33-35-37} sts.

Rnd 1: Knit around.

Repeat Rnd 1 once for Short Sleeve **or** until Sleeve measures approximately {5-5½}{6-6½-7}"/ {12.5-14}{15-16.5-18} cm from underarm for Long Sleeve.

RIBBING

Change to smaller size needles.

Row 1: K1, (P1, K1) around to last 2 sts, P2 tog: {28-28}{32-34-36} sts.

Rows 2 and 3: (K1, P1) around.

Bind off all sts **loosely** in ribbing.

Repeat for second sleeve.

Sew buttons to Front Flap, corresponding to buttonholes on Back Flap.

LITTLE HEARTS HAT
Ribbing

With smaller size needles, cast on {64-68}{72-76-80} sts.

Slip one-fourth of the sts onto **each** of 4 smaller size double-pointed needles; place a split-ring marker to indicate the beginning of the round.

Rnds 1-8: (K1, P1) around.

Body

Change to larger size needles.

Rnds 1-6: Knit around.

Rnd 7: K3, P1, ★ knit {15-16}{17-18-19} sts, P1; repeat from ★ 2 times **more**, knit around.

Rnd 8: Knit around.

Rnd 9: K2, P3, ★ knit {13-14}{15-16-17} sts, P3; repeat from ★ 2 times **more**, knit around.

Rnd 10: Knit around.

Rnd 11: K1, P5, ★ knit {11-12}{13-14-15} sts, P5; repeat from ★ 2 times **more**, knit around.

Rnd 12: Knit around.

Rnd 13: ★ P7, knit {9-10}{11-12-13} sts; repeat from ★ around.

Rnd 14: Knit around.

Rnd 15: ★ P3, K1, P3, knit {9-10}{11-12-13} sts; repeat from ★ around.

Rnd 16: Knit around.

Rnd 17: K1, P1, K3, P1, ★ knit {11-12}{13-14-15} sts, P1, K3, P1; repeat from ★ 2 times **more**, knit around.

Knit every round until Hat measures approximately {4½-5}{5½-6-6½}"/{11.5-12.5}{14-15-16.5} cm from cast on edge.

SHAPING

Rnd 1: (K2, K2 tog) around: {48-51}{54-57-60} sts.

Rnd 2: Knit around.

Rnd 3: (K1, K2 tog) around: {32-34}{36-38-40} sts.

Rnd 4: Knit around.

Rnd 5: K2 tog around: {16-17}{18-19-20} sts.

Rnd 6: Knit around.

Rnd 7: Knit {0-1}{0-1-0} st(s) *(see Zeros, page 58)*, K2 tog around: {8-9}{9-10-10} sts.

Cut yarn leaving a 12" (30.5 cm) length for sewing.

Thread yarn needle with long end and slip sts onto yarn needle; gather **tightly** to close and secure end.

Sew pom-pom to top of Hat.

● ● ● ○ INTERMEDIATE

DIAMOND BROCADE

SIZE INFORMATION

Finished Chest Circumference:
{15½-16½}{18¼-18¼-20}"/
{39.5-42}{46.5-46.5-51} cm

Finished Head Circumference:
{14¼-15}{16½-17-17¼}"/
{36-38}{42-43-44} cm

Size Note: We have printed the instructions for the sizes in different colors to make it easier for you to find.

- 0-3 months in Blue
- 3-6 months in Pink
- 6-9 months in Green
- 9-12 months in Red
- 12-18 months in Purple

Instructions in Black apply to all sizes.

SHOPPING LIST

Yarn (Medium Weight) [MEDIUM 4]
[5 ounces, 250 yards
(141 grams, 228 meters) per skein]:
☐ 2 skeins

Knitting Needles
Double-pointed (set of 5),
☐ Size 6 (4 mm) **and**
☐ Size 8 (5 mm)
   or sizes needed for gauge
Straight,
☐ Size 8 (5 mm) (for Leg Bands)

Note: A 36" (91.5 cm) circular needle may be used for the Magic Loop Method

Additional Supplies
☐ Split-ring marker
☐ Stitch markers
☐ Scrap yarn (to use as st holders)
☐ Yarn needle
☐ ¹¹⁄₁₆" (18 mm) Buttons - 3
☐ Purchased pom-pom
☐ Sewing needle & matching thread

GAUGE INFORMATION
With larger size needles,
   in Stockinette Stitch
   (knit every round),
   18 sts and 24 rnds = 4" (10 cm)

STITCH GUIDE
DOUBLE INCREASE (uses one st)
(K, YO, K) **all** in the st indicated.

TECHNIQUES USED
- YO *(Fig. 3a, page 58)*
- kfb *(Figs. 4a & b, page 59)*
- K2 tog *(Fig. 5, page 59)*
- P2 tog *(Fig. 6, page 59)*

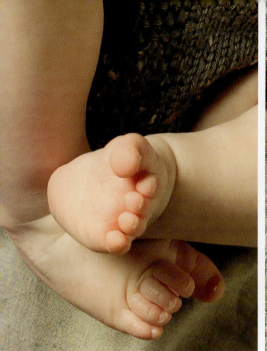

ONESIE

IMPORTANT! In order for the baby's head to fit through the neck opening, your stitches must be cast on with two larger size needles held together. Then slide the extra needle out and divide the stitches evenly onto four smaller double-pointed needles, or in half for the Magic Loop Method.

Onesie is worked in one piece from the Neck down.

Yoke
NECK RIBBING

Cast on {44-48}{52-56-60} sts. Slip one-fourth of the sts onto **each** of 4 smaller size double-pointed needles *(see Double-Pointed Needles, page 57)*; place a split-ring marker to indicate the beginning of the round *(see Markers, page 57)*.

Rnds 1-4: (K1, P1) around.

SHORT ROW SHAPING
Change to larger size needles.

Foundation Rnd: Knit around to last {4-4}{4-5-5} sts, place st marker, remove split-ring marker.

Row 1: Continuing to work in the same direction, double increase in next st, knit {6-6}{6-8-8} sts, double increase in next st, knit {14-16}{18-18-20} sts, double increase in next st, knit {6-6}{6-8-8} sts, double increase in next st, K1, place st marker, wrap & turn *(Fig. 10a, page 61)*.

Row 2: Purl across to next marker, remove st marker, P1, replace st marker, wrap & turn *(Fig. 10b, page 61)*.

Row 3: K2, double increase in next st, knit {8-8}{8-10-10} sts, double increase in next st, knit {16-18}{20-20-22} sts, double increase in next st, knit {8-8}{8-10-10} sts, double increase in next st, K2, remove st marker, knit next st **and** wrap together *(Fig. 10c, page 61)*, replace st marker, wrap & turn.

Row 4: Purl across to next st marker, remove st marker, purl next st **and** wrap together *(Fig. 10d, page 61)*, replace st marker, wrap & turn.

Row 5: K4, double increase in next st, knit {10-10}{10-12-12} sts, double increase in next st, knit {18-20}{22-22-24} sts, double increase in next st, knit {10-10}{10-12-12} sts, double increase in next st, K4, remove st marker, knit next st **and** wrap together, replace st marker, wrap & turn.

Row 6: Purl across to next st marker, remove st marker, purl next st **and** wrap together, replace st marker, wrap & turn.

0-3 months ONLY
Row 7: K6, double increase in next st, K 12, double increase in next st, K 20, double increase in next st, K 12, double increase in next st, K6, slip marker, knit next st **and** wrap together, do **not** turn.

Remaining 4 sizes ONLY
Row 7: K6, double increase in next st, knit {12}{12-14-14} sts, double increase in next st, knit {22}{24-24-26} sts, double increase in next st, knit {12}{12-14-14} sts, double increase in next st, K6, remove st marker, knit next st **and** wrap together, knit {0}{1-1-2} st(s) *(see Zeros, page 58)*, replace st marker, do **not** turn.

SLEEVE SHAPING - ALL SIZES
Foundation Rnd: Knit {2-3}{3-3-3} sts, kfb, knit {3-4}{5-5-6} sts, knit next st **and** wrap together, remove st marker, knit around to next st marker, remove st marker, place split-ring marker around next st (first st of Foundation Rnd) to mark beginning of rnd: {77-81}{85-89-93} sts.

Rnd 1: K3, P1, K1, P1, K3 (Rnd 1 of chart on page 28), place st marker, knit {7-8}{9-9-10} sts, double increase in next st (center st of previous double increase), knit {14-14}{14-16-16} sts, double increase in next st (center st of previous double increase), knit {22-24}{26-26-28} sts, double increase in next st (center st of previous double increase), knit {14-14}{14-16-16} sts, double increase in next st (center st of previous double increase), knit {7-8}{9-9-10} sts: {85-89}{93-97-101} sts.

27

Rnd 2: Work **next** rnd of chart to st marker, knit around.

Rnd 3: Work **next** rnd of chart to st marker, knit around working double increase in center st of each previous double increase: {93-97}{101-105-109} sts.

Repeat Rnds 2 and 3, {3-3}{4-4-5} times: {117-121}{133-137-149} sts.

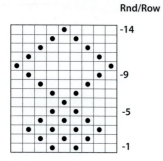

Repeat Rnds/Rows 1-14 for Diamond pattern

KEY
- ☐ knit on RS, purl on WS
- ● purl on RS, knit on WS

Body
Cut two, 14" (35.5 cm) lengths of scrap yarn to use as st holders.

Dividing Rnd: Work **next** rnd of chart to st marker, ★ knit across to center st of previous double increase, thread yarn needle with scrap yarn and slip the center st, the next {24-24}{26-28-30} sts, and the next center st onto scrap yarn (for Sleeve), cast 3 sts onto right needle using e-wrap method *(Fig. 2, page 58)*, place underarm marker; repeat from ★ once **more**, knit around: {71-75}{83-83-91} sts.

Rnd 1: Work **next** rnd of chart to st marker, knit around.

Repeat Rnd 1 until piece measures approximately {9-10}{11-12-12}"/{23-25.5}{28-30.5-30.5} cm from top of back neck.

Set-up Rnd: Work **next** rnd of chart to st marker, knit around to second underarm marker, remove marker; bind off next 3 sts, knit across to beginning marker, replace beginning marker with st marker, work **next** rnd of chart to next st marker, knit across to first underarm marker, remove marker; bind off next 3 sts, knit across remaining back sts: {32-34}{38-38-42} Back sts and {33-35}{39-39-43} Front sts.

Back Flap
Leaving Front sts on needle to be worked later, begin working in rows across Back sts.

Row 1 (Decrease row): P2 tog, purl across: {31-33}{37-37-41} sts.

Row 2 (Right side - Decrease row): K2 tog, knit across: {30-32}{36-36-40} sts.

Repeat Rows 1 and 2, {9-10}{12-12-14} times: 12 sts.

Next Row: Purl across.

Decrease Row: K5, K2 tog, K5: 11 sts.

BAND
Rows 1-3: Knit across.

Row 4 (Buttonhole row): K1, YO, K2 tog, (K2, YO, K2 tog) twice: 3 Buttonholes made.

Rows 5-7: Knit across.

Bind of all sts in **knit**.

Front Flap
With **wrong** side facing, attach yarn to beginning of Front sts. Maintain established pattern throughout, working chart between markers.

Rows 1 and 2: Bind off first {3-3}{3-3-4} sts, work across: {27-29}{33-33-35} sts.

0-3 months, 3-6 months, & 12-18 months ONLY

Rows 3 thru {5-5}{7}: Decrease, work across to last 2 sts, decrease: {21-23}{25} sts.

Row {6-6}{8} (Decrease row): K2 tog, work across to last 2 sts, K2 tog: {19-21}{23} sts.

Row {7-7}{9}: Purl across.

Repeat last 2 rows, {3-4}{5} times: 13 sts.

6-9 months & 9-12 months ONLY
Rows 3-6: Decrease, work across to last 2 sts, decrease: 25 sts.

Row 7: Purl across.

Row 8 (Decrease row): K2 tog, work across to last 2 sts, K2 tog: 23 sts.

Rows 9-19: Repeat Rows 7 and 8, 5 times; then repeat Row 7 once **more** removing markers: 13 sts.

All Sizes
Decrease Row: K4, K2 tog, K1, K2 tog, K4: 11 sts.

BAND
Rows 1-7: Knit across.

Bind off all sts in **knit**, leave last st on needle; do **not** cut yarn.

Leg Bands
LEFT
Slip remaining st onto straight needles and with **right** side facing, pick up {37-43}{49-53-55} sts along Left leg opening *(Figs. 11a & b, page 61)*: {38-44}{50-54-56} sts.

Rows 1 and 2: Knit across.

Bind off all sts in **knit**.

RIGHT
With **right** side facing and using straight needles, pick up {38-44}{50-54-56} sts along Right leg opening.

Rows 1 and 2: Knit across.

Bind off all sts in **knit**.

Sleeve

With **right** side facing and using larger size needles, pick up {3-3}{5-5-5} sts across cast on edge at underarm, knit across all sts of sleeve, removing scrap yarn and distributing sts evenly on needles to work in the round: {29-29}{33-35-37} sts.

Rnd 1: Knit around.

Repeat Rnd 1 once for Short Sleeve **or** until Sleeve measures approximately {5-5½}{6-6½-7}"/{12.5-14}{15-16.5-18} cm from underarm for Long Sleeve.

RIBBING

Change to smaller size needles.

Row 1: K1, (P1, K1) around to last 2 sts, P2 tog: {28-28}{32-34-36} sts.

Rows 2 and 3: (K1, P1) around.

Bind off all sts **loosely** in ribbing.

Repeat for second sleeve.

Sew buttons to Front Flap, corresponding to buttonholes on Back Flap.

HAT

Ribbing

With smaller size needles, cast on {64-68}{74-76-78} sts **loosely**.

Slip sts onto 4 double-pointed needles; place a split-ring marker to indicate the beginning of the round.

Rnd 1 (Right side): (K1, P1) around.

Repeat Rnd 1, 7 times **more** increasing {11-7}{6-4-2} sts evenly spaced on 7th round: {75-75}{80-80-80} sts.

Chart A

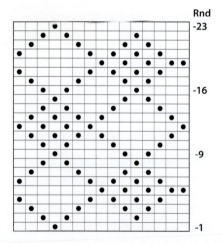

Chart B

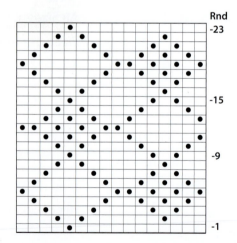

KEY

☐ knit on RS, purl on WS
● purl on RS, knit on WS

Body

Change to larger size needles.

0-3 months & 3-6 months ONLY

Rnds 1-23: Work Rnds 1-23 of Chart A.

6-9 months & 9-12 months ONLY

Rnds 1-30: Work Rnds 1-22 of Chart B once; then repeat Rnds 9-16 once **more**.

12-18 months ONLY

Rows 1-38: Work Rnds 1-23 of Chart B once; then repeat Rnds 9-23 once **more**.

All Sizes

Next {2-4}{2-4-2} Rnds: Knit around.

SHAPING

Rnd 1: ★ Knit {13-13}{6-6-6} sts, K2 tog; repeat from ★ around: 70 sts.

Rnd 2 AND ALL WRONG SIDE RNDS THROUGH RND 12: Knit around.

Rnd 3: (K5, K2 tog) around: 60 sts.

Rnd 5: (K4, K2 tog) around: 50 sts.

Rnd 7: (K3, K2 tog) around: 40 sts.

Rnd 9: (K2, K2 tog) around: 30 sts.

Rnd 11: (K1, K2 tog) around: 20 sts.

Rnd 13: K2 tog around: 10 sts.

Cut yarn leaving a 12" (30.5 cm) length for sewing.

Thread yarn needle with long end and slip sts onto yarn needle; gather **tightly** to close and secure end.

Sew pom-pom to top of Hat.

31

FRAMED CABLE

●●●○ **INTERMEDIATE**

SHOPPING LIST

Yarn (Medium Weight) [MEDIUM 4]
[5 ounces, 250 yards (141.7 grams, 228 meters) per skein]:
☐ 2 skeins

Knitting Needles

Double-pointed (set of 5),
☐ Size 6 (4 mm) **and**
☐ Size 8 (5 mm)
 or sizes needed for gauge
Straight,
☐ Size 8 (5 mm) (for Leg Bands)

Note: A 36" (91.5 cm) circular needle may be used for the Magic Loop Method

Additional Supplies

☐ Cable needle
☐ Split-ring marker
☐ Stitch markers
☐ Scrap yarn (to use as st holders and for provisional cast on)
☐ Size H (5 mm) crochet hook
☐ Yarn needle
☐ ¹¹/₁₆" (18 mm) Buttons - 3
☐ Sewing needle & matching thread

SIZE INFORMATION

Finished Chest Circumference:
{15½-16½}{18¼-18¼-20}"/
 {39.5-42}{46.5-46.5-51} cm

Finished Head Circumference:
{14¼-15}{16½-17-17¼}"/
 {36-38}{42-43-44} cm

Size Note: We have printed the instructions for the sizes in different colors to make it easier for you to find.

- 0-3 months in Blue
- 3-6 months in Pink
- 6-9 months in Green
- 9-12 months in Red
- 12-18 months in Purple

Instructions in Black apply to all sizes.

GAUGE INFORMATION

With larger size needles,
 in Stockinette Stitch (knit every round),
 18 sts and 24 rnds = 4" (10 cm)

STITCH GUIDE

DOUBLE INCREASE (uses one st) (K, YO, K) **all** in the st indicated.

RIGHT TWIST (uses next 2 sts)
Slip next st onto cable needle and hold in **back** of work, K1 from left needle, K1 from cable needle.

LEFT TWIST (uses next 2 sts)
Slip next st onto cable needle and hold in **front** of work, K1 from left needle, K1 from cable needle.

CABLE 6 BACK *(abbreviated C6B)*
 (uses 6 sts)
Slip next 3 sts onto cable needle and hold in **back** of work, K3 from left needle, K3 from cable needle.

TECHNIQUES USED

- YO *(Fig. 3a, page 58)*
- kfb *(Figs. 4a & b, page 59)*
- K2 tog *(Fig. 5, page 59)*
- P2 tog *(Fig. 6, page 59)*
- SSK *(Figs. 7a-c, page 59)*
- K3 tog *(Fig. 8, page 60)*

ONESIE

IMPORTANT! In order for the baby's head to fit through the neck opening, your stitches must be cast on with two larger size needles held together. Then slide the extra needle out and divide the stitches evenly onto four smaller double-pointed needles, or in half for the Magic Loop Method.

Onesie is worked in one piece from the Neck down.

Yoke

NECK RIBBING

Cast on {44-48}{52-56-60} sts. Slip one-fourth of the sts onto **each** of 4 smaller size double-pointed needles *(see Double-Pointed Needles, page 57)*; place a split-ring marker to indicate the beginning of the round *(see Markers, page 57)*.

Rnds 1-4: (K1, P1) around.

SHORT ROW SHAPING

Change to larger size needles.

Foundation Rnd: Knit around to last {4-4}{4-5-5} sts, place st marker, remove split-ring marker.

Row 1: Continuing to work in the same direction, double increase in next st, knit {6-6}{6-8-8} sts, double increase in next st, knit {14-16}{18-18-20} sts, double increase in next st, knit {6-6}{6-8-8} sts, double increase in next st, K1, place st marker, wrap & turn *(Fig. 10a, page 61)*.

Row 2: Purl across to next marker, remove st marker, P1, replace st marker, wrap & turn *(Fig. 10b, page 61)*.

Row 3: K2, double increase in next st, knit {8-8}{8-10-10} sts, double increase in next st, knit {16-18}{20-20-22} sts, double increase in next st, knit {8-8}{8-10-10} sts, double increase in next st, K2, remove st marker, knit next st **and** wrap together *(Fig. 10c, page 61)*, replace st marker, wrap & turn.

Row 4: Purl across to next st marker, remove st marker, purl next st **and** wrap together *(Fig. 10d, page 61)*, replace st marker, wrap & turn.

Row 5: K4, double increase in next st, knit {10-10}{10-12-12} sts, double increase in next st, knit {18-20}{22-22-24} sts, double increase in next st, knit {10-10}{10-12-12} sts, double increase in next st, K4, remove st marker, knit next st **and** wrap together, replace st marker, wrap & turn.

Row 6: Purl across to next st marker, remove st marker, purl next st **and** wrap together, replace st marker, wrap & turn.

Row 7: K6, double increase in next st, knit {12-12}{12-14-14} sts, double increase in next st, knit {20-22}{24-24-26} sts, double increase in next st, knit {12-12}{12-14-14} sts, double increase in next st, K6, remove st marker, knit next st **and** wrap together, knit {0-1}{2-2-3} sts *(see Zeros, page 58)*, replace st marker, do **not** turn.

SLEEVE SHAPING

Foundation Rnd: Kfb, K1, kfb twice, K1, kfb, knit {0-1}{2-2-3} sts, knit next st **and** wrap together, remove st marker, knit across to next st marker: {80-84}{88-92-96} sts.

Rnd 1: Remove st marker, slip one st from right needle to left needle, replace st marker (indicating beginning of rnd), slip the st from the left needle **back** to the right needle, RT, K6, LT, knit {8-9}{10-10-11} sts, double increase in next st, knit {14-14}{14-16-16} sts, double increase in next st, knit {22-24}{26-26-28} sts, double increase in next st, knit {14-14}{14-16-16} sts, double increase in next st, knit {7-8}{9-9-10} sts: {88-92}{96-100-104} sts.

Rnd 2: K2, P1, K6, P1, knit around.

Rnd 3: Remove st marker, slip one st from right needle to left needle, replace st marker (indicating beginning of rnd), slip the st from the left needle **back** to the right needle, RT, P1, K6, P1, LT, knit {8-9}{10-10-11} sts, double increase in next st, knit {16-16}{16-18-18} sts, double increase in next st, knit {24-26}{28-28-30} sts, double increase in next st, knit {16-16}{16-18-18} sts, double increase in next st, knit {7-8}{9-9-10} sts: {96-100}{104-108-112} sts.

Rnd 4: K2, P2, K6, P2, knit around.

Rnd 5: Remove st marker, slip one st from right needle to left needle, replace st marker (indicating beginning of rnd), slip the st from the left needle **back** to the right needle, RT, P2, C6B, P2, knit {10-11}{12-12-13} sts, double increase in next st, knit {18-18}{18-20-20} sts, double increase in next st, knit {26-28}{30-30-32} sts, double increase in next st, knit {18-18}{18-20-20} sts, double increase in next st, knit {7-8}{9-9-10} sts: {104-108}{112-116-120} sts.

Rnd 6: K2, P3, K6, P3, knit around.

St marker now indicates the beginning of the Cable pattern in addition to the beginning of the rnd.

Rnd 7: RT, P3, K6, P3, LT (Rnd 7 on chart below), place st marker, knit {8-9}{10-10-11} sts, double increase in next st (center st of previous double increase), knit {20-20}{20-22-22} sts, double increase in next st (center st of previous double increase), knit {28-30}{32-32-34} sts, double increase in next st (center st of previous double increase), knit {20-20}{20-22-22} sts, double increase in next st (center st of previous double increase), knit {8-9}{10-10-11} sts: {112-116}{120-124-128} sts.

Rnd 8: Work **next** rnd of chart to marker, knit around.

Rnd 9: Work **next** rnd of chart to marker, knit around working double increase in center st of each previous double increase: {120-124}{128-132-136} sts.

Repeat Rnds 8 and 9, {0-0}{1-1-2} time(s): {120-124}{136-140-152} sts.

Body

Cut two, 14" (35.5 cm) lengths of scrap yarn to use as st holders.

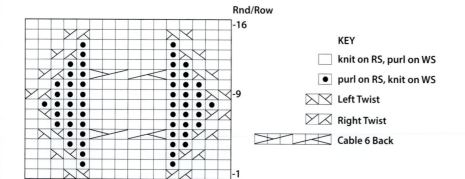

Repeat Rnds/Rows 1-16 for Diamond pattern

KEY
☐ knit on RS, purl on WS
● purl on RS, knit on WS
⧄⧅ Left Twist
⧅⧄ Right Twist
⟆⟅ Cable 6 Back

Dividing Rnd: Work **next** rnd of chart to marker, ★ knit across to center st of previous double increase, thread yarn needle with scrap yarn and slip the center st, the next {24-24}{26-28-30} sts, and the next center st onto scrap yarn (for Sleeve), cast 3 sts onto right needle using e-wrap method *(Fig. 2, page 58)*, place underarm marker; repeat from ★ once **more**, knit around: {74-78}{86-86-94} sts.

Rnd 1: Work **next** rnd of chart to marker, knit around.

Repeat Rnd 1 until piece measures approximately {9-10}{11-12-12}"/ {23-25.5}{28-30.5-30.5} cm from top of back neck, ending by working an odd-numbered rnd of chart.

Set-up Rnd: Work **next** rnd of chart to marker, knit around to second underarm marker, remove marker; bind off next 3 sts, knit across to beginning marker, work **next** rnd of chart to marker, knit across to first underarm marker, remove marker; bind off next 3 sts, knit across remaining back sts: {32-34}{38-38-42} Back sts and {36-38}{42-42-46} Front sts.

Back Flap

Leaving Front sts on needle to be worked later, begin working in rows across Back sts.

Row 1 (Decrease row): P2 tog, purl across: {31-33}{37-37-41} sts.

Row 2 (Right side - Decrease row): K2 tog, knit across: {30-32}{36-36-40} sts.

Repeat Rows 1 and 2, {9-10}{12-12-14} times: 12 sts.

Next Row: Purl across.

Decrease Row: K5, K2 tog, K5: 11 sts.

BAND
Rows 1-3: Knit across.

Row 4 (Buttonhole row): K1, YO, K2 tog, (K2, YO, K2 tog) twice: 3 Buttonholes made.

Rows 5-7: Knit across.

Bind of all sts in **knit**.

Front Flap

With **wrong** side facing, attach yarn to beginning of Front sts. Maintain established pattern throughout, working Chart between markers.

Rows 1 and 2: Bind off first {3-3}{3-3-4} sts, work across: {30-32}{36-36-38} sts.

0-3 months, 3-6 months, & 12-18 months ONLY
Rows 3 thru {5-5}{7}: Decrease, work across to last 2 sts, decrease: {24-26}{28} sts.

Row {6-6}{8} (Decrease row): K2 tog, work across to last 2 sts, K2 tog: {22-24}{26} sts.

Row {7-7}{9}: Purl across.

Repeat last 2 rows, {3-4}{5} times: 16 sts.

6-9 months & 9-12 months ONLY
Rows 3-6: Decrease, work across to last 2 sts, decrease: 28 sts.

Row 7: Purl across.

Row 8 (Decrease row): K2 tog, work across to last 2 sts, K2 tog: 26 sts.

Rows 9-19: Repeat Rows 7 and 8, 5 times; then repeat Row 7 once **more** removing markers: 16 sts.

All Sizes
Decrease Row: K2, K2 tog twice, K1, K2 tog, K1, K2 tog twice, K2: 11 sts.

BAND
Rows 1-7: Knit across.

Bind off all sts in **knit**; leave last st on needle; do **not** cut yarn.

Leg Bands
LEFT
Slip remaining st onto straight needles and with **right** side facing, pick up {37-43}{49-53-55} sts along Left leg opening *(Figs. 11a & b, page 61)*: {38-44}{50-54-56} sts.

Rows 1 and 2: Knit across.

Bind off all sts in **knit**.

RIGHT

With **right** side facing and using straight needles, pick up {38-44}{50-54-56} sts along Right leg opening.

Rows 1 and 2: Knit across.

Bind off all sts in **knit**.

Sleeve

With **right** side facing and using larger size needles, pick up {3-3}{5-5-5} sts across cast on edge at underarm, knit across all sts of sleeve, removing scrap yarn and distributing sts evenly on needles to work in the round: {29-29}{33-35-37} sts.

Rnd 1: Knit around.

Repeat Rnd 1 once for Short Sleeve **or** until Sleeve measures approximately {5-5½}{6-6½-7}"/{12.5-14}{15-16.5-18} cm from underarm for Long Sleeve.

RIBBING

Change to smaller size needles.

Row 1: K1, (P1, K1) around to last 2 sts, P2 tog: {28-28}{32-34-36} sts.

Rows 2 and 3: (K1, P1) around.

Bind off all sts **loosely** in ribbing.

Repeat for second sleeve.

Sew buttons to Front Flap, corresponding to buttonholes on Back Flap.

CABLED TAM
Band

With larger size needles and leaving a long tail for grafting, cast on 12 sts using provisional cast *(Fig. A)*.

Fig. A

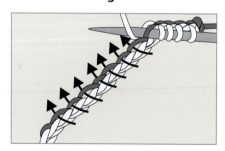

Row 1: K1, P1, K1, P6, K1, P1, K1.

Row 2 (Right side): P1, K1, P1, K6, P1, K1, P1.

Rows 3-5: Repeat Rows 1 and 2 once, then repeat Row 1 once **more**.

Row 6: P1, K1, P1, C6B, P1, K1, P1.

Repeat Rows 1-6, {13-14}{15-16-17} times; then repeat Rows 1 and 2 once **more**: {14-15}{16-17-18} Cables.

Do **not** cut yarn.

Slip sts from provisional cast on onto another needle. Using the long tail left from the cast on, graft ends of band together *(Figs. 12a & b, page 62)*.

Body

With **right** side facing and using larger size needles, pick up {84-90}{90-96-96} sts evenly spaced around Band; slip sts onto **each** of 4 double-pointed needles; place a split-ring marker to indicate the beginning of the round.

Rnd 1: Knit around.

Repeat Rnd 1 for Stockinette Stitch until piece measures approximately {3-3}{3¼-3¼-3½}"/{7.5-7.5}{8.5-8.5-9} cm from bottom edge of Band, placing a st marker every {14-15}{15-16-16} sts on last rnd.

SHAPING

Decrease Rnd: ★ Knit across to within 2 sts of next marker, SSK; repeat from ★ around: {78-84}{84-90-90} sts.

Repeat Decrease Rnd until 12 sts remain.

Last Decrease Rnd: SSK around removing markers: 6 sts.

Cut yarn leaving a 12" (30.5 cm) length for sewing.

Thread yarn needle with long end and slip sts onto yarn needle; gather **tightly** to close and secure end.

Bobble

With larger size needles, cast on one stitch; (K1, YO, K1, YO, K1) **all** into this st: 5 sts.

Row 1 (Wrong side)**:** Purl across.

Row 2: Knit across.

Rows 3 and 4: Repeat Rows 1 and 2.

Row 5: P2 tog, P1, P2 tog: 3 sts.

Row 6: K3 tog: one st.

Cut yarn leaving an 8" (20.5 cm) length for sewing; bring yarn end through remaining st to tighten.

Using ends of yarn, attach Bobble to top of Tam.

LACE ACCENT

SIZE INFORMATION

Finished Chest Circumference:
{15½-16½}{18¼-18¼-20}"/
{39.5-42}{46.5-46.5-51} cm

Finished Head Circumference:
{14¼-15}{16½-17-17¼}"/
{36-38}{42-43-44} cm

Size Note: We have printed the instructions for the sizes in different colors to make it easier for you to find.

- 0-3 months in Blue
- 3-6 months in Pink
- 6-9 months in Green
- 9-12 months in Red
- 12-18 months in Purple

Instructions in Black apply to all sizes.

●●●○ **INTERMEDIATE**

SHOPPING LIST

Yarn (Medium Weight)
[4 ounces, 203 yards
(113 grams, 186 meters) per skein]:
☐ 2 skeins

Knitting Needles
Double-pointed (set of 5),
☐ Size 6 (4 mm) **and**
☐ Size 8 (5 mm)
   or sizes needed for gauge
Straight,
☐ Size 8 (5 mm) (for Leg Bands)

Note: A 36" (91.5 cm) circular needle may be used for the Magic Loop Method

Additional Supplies
☐ Split-ring marker
☐ Stitch markers
☐ Scrap yarn (to use as st holders)
☐ Yarn needle
☐ ¹¹⁄₁₆" (18 mm) Buttons - 3
☐ Purchased pom-pom
☐ Sewing needle & matching thread

GAUGE INFORMATION
With larger size needles,
   in Stockinette Stitch
   (knit every round),
   18 sts and 24 rnds = 4" (10 cm)

STITCH GUIDE
DOUBLE INCREASE (uses one st)
(YO, K, YO) **all** in the st indicated.

TECHNIQUES USED
- **YO** *(Figs. 3a-c, pages 58 & 59)*
- **kfb** *(Figs. 4a & b, page 59)*
- **K2 tog** *(Fig. 5, page 59)*
- **P2 tog** *(Fig. 6, page 59)*
- **Slip 2 tog, K1, P2SSO** *(Figs. 9a & b, page 60)*

ONESIE

IMPORTANT! In order for the baby's head to fit through the neck opening, your stitches must be cast on with two larger size needles held together. Then slide the extra needle out and divide the stitches evenly onto four smaller double-pointed needles, or in half for the Magic Loop Method.

Onesie is worked in one piece from the Neck down.

Yoke

NECK RIBBING

Cast on {44-48}{52-56-60} sts. Slip one-fourth of the sts onto **each** of 4 smaller size double-pointed needles *(see Double-Pointed Needles, page 57)*; place a split-ring marker to indicate the beginning of the round *(see Markers, page 57)*.

Rnds 1-4: (K1, P1) around.

SHORT ROW SHAPING

Change to larger size needles.

Foundation Rnd: Knit around to last {4-4}{4-5-5} sts, place st marker, remove split-ring marker.

Row 1: Continuing to work in the same direction, double increase in next st, knit {6-6}{6-8-8} sts, double increase in next st, knit {14-16}{18-18-20} sts, double increase in next st, knit {6-6}{6-8-8} sts, double increase in next st, K1, place st marker, wrap & turn *(Fig. 10a, page 61)*.

Row 2: Purl across to next marker, remove st marker, P1, replace st marker, wrap & turn *(Fig. 10b, page 61)*.

Row 3: K2, double increase in next st, knit {8-8}{8-10-10} sts, double increase in next st, knit {16-18}{20-20-22} sts, double increase in next st, knit {8-8}{8-10-10} sts, double increase in next st, K2, remove st marker, knit next st **and** wrap together *(Fig. 10c, page 61)*, replace st marker, wrap & turn.

Row 4: Purl across to next st marker, remove st marker, purl next st **and** wrap together *(Fig. 10d, page 61)*, replace st marker, wrap & turn.

Row 5: K4, double increase in next st, knit {10-10}{10-12-12} sts, double increase in next st, knit {18-20}{22-22-24} sts, double increase in next st, knit {10-10}{10-12-12} sts, double increase in next st, K4, remove st marker, knit next st **and** wrap together, replace st marker, wrap & turn.

Row 6: Purl across to next st marker, remove st marker, purl next st **and** wrap together, replace st marker, wrap & turn.

0-3 months ONLY
Row 7: K6, double increase in next st, K 12, double increase in next st, K 20, double increase in next st, K 12, double increase in next st, K6, slip marker, knit next st **and** wrap together, do **not** turn.

Remaining 4 sizes ONLY
Row 7: K6, double increase in next st, knit {12}{12-14-14} sts, double increase in next st, knit {22}{24-24-26} sts, double increase in next st, knit {12}{12-14-14} sts, double increase in next st, K6, remove st marker, knit next st **and** wrap together, knit {0}{1-1-2} st(s) *(see Zeros, page 58)*, replace st marker, do **not** turn.

SLEEVE SHAPING - ALL SIZES
Foundation Rnd: Knit {2-3}{3-3-3} sts, kfb, knit {3-4}{5-5-6} sts, knit next st **and** wrap together, remove st marker, knit around to next st marker, remove st marker, place split-ring marker around next st (first st of Foundation Rnd) to mark beginning of rnd: {77-81}{85-89-93} sts.

Rnd 1: YO, P3, slip 2 tog, K1, P2SSO, P3, YO (Rnd 1 on chart below), place st marker, knit {7-8}{9-9-10} sts, double increase in next st (center st of previous double increase), knit {14-14}{14-16-16} sts, double increase in next st (center st of previous double increase), knit {22-24}{26-26-28} sts, double increase in next st (center st of previous double increase), knit {14-14}{14-16-16} sts, double increase in next st (center st of previous double increase), knit {7-8}{9-9-10} sts: {85-89} {93-97-101} sts.

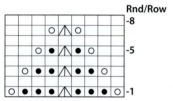

Repeat Rnds/Rows 1-8 for Lace pattern

KEY
- knit on RS, purl on WS
- purl on RS, knit on WS
- slip 2, K1, P2SSO

Rnd 2: Work **next** rnd of chart to st marker, knit around.

Rnd 3: Work **next** rnd of chart to st marker, knit around working double increase in center st of each previous double increase: {93-97} {101-105-109} sts.

Repeat Rnds 2 and 3, {3-3} {4-4-5} times: {117-121} {133-137-149} sts.

Body

Cut two, 14" (35.5 cm) lengths of scrap yarn to use as st holders.

Dividing Rnd: Work **next** rnd of chart to st marker, ★ knit across to center st of previous double increase, thread yarn needle with scrap yarn and slip the center st, the next {24-24} {26-28-30} sts, and the next center st onto scrap yarn (for Sleeve), cast 3 sts onto right needle using e-wrap method *(Fig. 2, page 58)*, place underarm marker; repeat from ★ once **more**, knit around: {71-75} {83-83-91} sts.

Rnd 1: Work **next** rnd of chart to st marker, knit around.

Repeat Rnd 1 until piece measures approximately {9-10}{11-12-12}"/ {23-25.5}{28-30.5-30.5} cm from top of back neck, ending by working an odd-numbered rnd of chart.

Set-up Rnd: Work **next** rnd of chart to st marker, knit around to second underarm marker, remove marker; bind off next 3 sts, knit across to beginning marker, replace beginning marker with st marker, work **next** rnd of chart to next st marker, knit across to first underarm marker, remove marker; bind off next 3 sts, knit across remaining back sts: {32-34} {38-38-42} Back sts and {33-35} {39-39-43} Front sts.

Back Flap

Leaving Front sts on needle to be worked later, begin working in rows across Back sts.

Row 1 (Decrease row): P2 tog, purl across: {31-33}{37-37-41} sts.

Row 2 (Right side - Decrease row): K2 tog, knit across: {30-32} {36-36-40} sts.

Repeat Rows 1 and 2, {9-10} {12-12-14} times: 12 sts.

Next Row: Purl across.

Decrease Row: K5, K2 tog, K5: 11 sts.

BAND
Rows 1-3: Knit across.

Row 4 (Buttonhole row): K1, YO, K2 tog, (K2, YO, K2 tog) twice: 3 Buttonholes made.
Rows 5-7: Knit across.

Bind of all sts in **knit**.

Front Flap

With **wrong** side facing, attach yarn to beginning of Front sts. Maintain established pattern throughout, working Chart between markers.

Rows 1 and 2: Bind off first {3-3} {3-3-4} sts, work across: {27-29} {33-33-35} sts.

0-3 months, 3-6 months, & 12-18 months ONLY
Rows 3 thru {5-5}{7}: Decrease, work across to last 2 sts, decrease: {21-23}{25} sts.

Row {6-6}{8} (Decrease row): K2 tog, work across to last 2 sts, K2 tog: {19-21}{23} sts.

Row {7-7}{9}: Purl across.

Repeat last 2 rows, {3-4}{5} times: 13 sts.

6-9 months & 9-12 months ONLY
Rows 3-6: Decrease, work across to last 2 sts, decrease: 25 sts.

Row 7: Purl across.

Row 8 (Decrease row): K2 tog, work across to last 2 sts, K2 tog: 23 sts.

Rows 9-19: Repeat Rows 7 and 8, 5 times; then repeat Row 7 once **more** removing markers: 13 sts.

All Sizes
Decrease Row: K5, slip 2, K1, P2SSO, K5: 11 sts.

BAND
Rows 1-7: Knit across.

Bind off all sts in **knit**, leave last st on needle; do **not** cut yarn.

Leg Bands
LEFT
Slip remaining st onto straight needles and with **right** side facing, pick up {37-43}{49-53-55} sts along Left leg opening *(Figs. 11a & b, page 61)*: {38-44}{50-54-56} sts.

Rows 1 and 2: Knit across.

Bind off all sts in **knit**.

RIGHT

With **right** side facing and using straight needles, pick up {38-44}{50-54-56} sts along Right leg opening.

Rows 1 and 2: Knit across.

Bind off all sts in **knit**.

Sleeve

With **right** side facing and using larger size needles, pick up {3-3}{5-5-5} sts across cast on edge at underarm, knit across all sts of sleeve, removing scrap yarn and distributing sts evenly on needles to work in the round: {29-29}{33-35-37} sts.

Rnd 1: Knit around.

Repeat Rnd 1 once for Short Sleeve **or** until Sleeve measures approximately {5-5½}{6-6½-7}"/{12.5-14}{15-16.5-18} cm from underarm for Long Sleeve.

RIBBING

Change to smaller size needles.

Row 1: K1, (P1, K1) around to last 2 sts, P2 tog: {28-28}{32-34-36} sts.

Rows 2 and 3: (K1, P1) around.

Bind off all sts **loosely** in ribbing.

Repeat for second sleeve.

Sew buttons to Front Flap, corresponding to buttonholes on Back Flap.

ROLLED BRIM HAT

With larger size needles, cast on {64-68}{72-76-80} sts.

Slip sts onto 4 double-pointed needles; place a split-ring marker to indicate the beginning of the round.

Rnd 1 (Right side)**:** Knit around.

Repeat Rnd 1 until Hat measures approximately {4½-5}{5½-6-6½}"/{11.5-12.5}{14-15-16.5} cm from cast on edge.

SHAPING

Rnd 1: (K2, K2 tog) around: {48-51}{54-57-60} sts.

Rnd 2: Knit around.

Rnd 3: (K1, K2 tog) around: {32-34}{36-38-40} sts.

Rnd 4: Knit around.

Rnd 5: K2 tog around: {16-17}{18-19-20} sts.

Rnd 6: Knit around.

Rnd 7: Knit {0-1}{0-1-0} st(s), K2 tog around: {8-9}{9-10-10} sts.

Cut yarn leaving a 12" (30.5 cm) length for sewing.

Thread yarn needle with long end and slip sts onto yarn needle; gather **tightly** to close and secure end.

Sew pom-pom to top of Hat.

● ● ● ○ INTERMEDIATE

SHOPPING LIST

Yarn (Medium Weight) [MEDIUM 4]
[3.5 ounces, 180 yards
(100 grams, 165 meters) per skein]:
☐ 2 skeins

Knitting Needles
Double-pointed (set of 5),
☐ Size 6 (4 mm) **and**
☐ Size 8 (5 mm)
  or sizes needed for gauge
Straight,
☐ Size 8 (5 mm) (for Leg Bands)

Note: A 36" (91.5 cm) circular needle may be used for the Magic Loop Method

Additional Supplies
☐ Split-ring marker
☐ Stitch markers
☐ Scrap yarn (to use as st holders)
☐ Yarn needle
☐ ¹¹/₁₆" (18 mm) Buttons - 3
☐ Sewing needle & matching thread

48   www.leisurearts.com

MIXED BERRY

SIZE INFORMATION

Finished Chest Circumference:
{15½-16½}{18¼-18¼-20}"/
{39.5-42}{46.5-46.5-51} cm

Finished Head Circumference:
{14¼-15}{16½-17-17¼}"/
{36-38}{42-43-44} cm

Size Note: We have printed the instructions for the sizes in different colors to make it easier for you to find.

• 0-3 months in Blue
• 3-6 months in Pink
• 6-9 months in Green
• 9-12 months in Red
• 12-18 months in Purple

Instructions in Black apply to all sizes.

GAUGE INFORMATION
With larger size needles,
  in Stockinette Stitch
  (knit every round),
  18 sts and 24 rnds= 4" (10 cm)

STITCH GUIDE
DOUBLE INCREASE (uses one st)
(K, YO, K) **all** in the st indicated.

TECHNIQUES USED
• YO *(Fig. 3a, page 58)*
• K2 tog *(Fig. 5, page 59)*
• P2 tog *(Fig. 6, page 59)*

ONESIE

IMPORTANT! In order for the baby's head to fit through the neck opening, your stitches must be cast on with two larger size needles held together. Then slide the extra needle out and divide the stitches evenly onto four smaller double-pointed needles, or in half for the Magic Loop Method.

Onsie is worked in one piece from the Neck down.

Yoke
NECK RIBBING

Cast on {44-48}{52-56-60} sts. Slip one-fourth of the sts onto **each of 4 smaller size double-pointed needles *(see Double-Pointed Needles, page 57)*;** place a split-ring marker to indicate the beginning of the round *(see Markers, page 57)*.

Rnds 1-4: (K1, P1) around.

SHORT ROW SHAPING
Change to larger size needles.

Foundation Rnd: Knit around to last {4-4}{4-5-5} sts, place st marker, remove split-ring marker.

Row 1: Continuing to work in the same direction, double increase in next st, knit {6-6}{6-8-8} sts, double increase in next st, knit {14-16}{18-18-20} sts, double increase in next st, knit {6-6}{6-8-8} sts, double increase in next st, K1, place st marker, wrap & turn *(Fig. 10a, page 61)*.

Row 2: Purl across to next marker, remove st marker, P1, replace st marker, wrap & turn *(Fig. 10b, page 61)*.

Row 3: K2, double increase in next st, knit {8-8}{8-10-10} sts, double increase in next st, knit {16-18}{20-20-22} sts, double increase in next st, knit {8-8}{8-10-10} sts, double increase in next st, K2, remove st marker, knit next st **and** wrap together *(Fig. 10c, page 61)*, replace st marker, wrap & turn.

Row 4: Purl across to next st marker, remove st marker, purl next st **and** wrap together *(Fig. 10d, page 61)*, replace st marker, wrap & turn.

Row 5: K4, double increase in next st, knit {10-10}{10-12-12} sts, double increase in next st, knit {18-20}{22-22-24} sts, double increase in next st,

50   www.leisurearts.com

knit {10-10}{10-12-12} sts, double increase in next st, K4, remove st marker, knit next st **and** wrap together, replace st marker, wrap & turn.

Row 6: Purl across to next st marker, remove st marker, purl next st **and** wrap together, replace st marker, wrap & turn.

Row 7: K6, double increase in next st, knit {12-12}{12-14-14} sts, double increase in next st, knit {20-22}{24-24-26} sts, double increase in next st, knit {12-12}{12-14-14} sts, double increase in next st, K6, remove st marker, knit next st **and** wrap together, replace st marker, do **not** turn.

SLEEVE SHAPING

Foundation Rnd: Knit {6-8}{10-10-12} sts, knit next st **and** wrap together, remove st marker, knit around to next st marker, remove st marker, place split-ring marker around next st (first st of Foundation Rnd) to mark beginning of rnd: {76-80}{84-88-92} sts.

Rnd 1: Knit {14-16}{18-18-20} sts, double increase in next st (center st of previous double increase), knit {14-14}{14-16-16} sts, double increase in next st (center st of previous double increase), knit {22-24}{26-26-28} sts, double increase in next st (center st of previous double increase), knit {14-14}{14-16-16} sts, double increase in next st (center st of previous double increase), K8: {84-88}{92-96-100} sts.

Rnd 2: Knit around.

Rnd 3: Knit around working double increase in center st of each previous double increase: {92-96}{100-104-108} sts.

Repeat Rnds 2 and 3, {3-3}{4-4-5} times: {116-120}{132-136-148} sts.

Body

Cut two, 14" (35.5 cm) lengths of scrap yarn to use as st holders.

Dividing Rnd: ★ Knit across to center st of previous double increase, thread yarn needle with scrap yarn and slip the center st, the next {24-24}{26-28-30} sts, and the next center st onto scrap yarn (for Sleeve), cast 3 sts onto right needle using e-wrap method *(Fig. 2, page 58)*, place underarm marker; repeat from ★ once **more**, knit around: {70-74}{82-82-90} sts.

Rnd 1: Knit around.

Repeat Rnd 1 until piece measures approximately {9-10}{11-12-12}"/ {23-25.5}{28-30.5-30.5} cm from top of back neck.

Set-up Rnd: Knit around to second underarm marker, remove marker; bind off next 3 sts, knit across to beginning marker, remove marker, knit across to first underarm marker, remove marker; bind off next 3 sts, knit across remaining back sts: {32-34}{38-38-42} Back sts and {32-34}{38-38-42} Front sts.

Back Flap

Leaving Front sts on needle to be worked later, begin working in rows across Back sts.

Row 1 (Decrease row): P2 tog, purl across: {31-33}{37-37-41} sts.

Row 2 (Right side - Decrease row): K2 tog, knit across: {30-32}{36-36-40} sts.

Repeat Rows 1 and 2, {9-10}{12-12-14} times: 12 sts.

Next Row: Purl across.

Decrease Row: K5, K2 tog, K5: 11 sts.

BAND

Rows 1-3: Knit across.

Row 4 (Buttonhole row): K1, YO, K2 tog, (K2, YO, K2 tog) twice: 3 Buttonholes made.

Rows 5-7: Knit across.

Bind of all sts in **knit**.

Front Flap

With **wrong** side facing, attach yarn to beginning of Front sts. Maintain established pattern throughout.

Rows 1 and 2: Bind off first {3-3}{3-3-4} sts, work across: {26-28}{32-32-34} sts.

0-3 months, 3-6 months, & 12-18 months ONLY

Rows 3 thru {5-5}{7}: Decrease, work across to last 2 sts, decrease: {20-22}{24} sts.

Row {6-6}{8} (Decrease row): K2 tog, knit across to last 2 sts, K2 tog: {18-20}{22} sts.

Row {7-7}{9}: Purl across.

Repeat last 2 rows, {3-4}{5} times: 12 sts.

6-9 months & 9-12 months ONLY

Rows 3-6: Decrease, work across to last 2 sts, decrease: 24 sts.

Row 7: Purl across.

Row 8 (Decrease row): K2 tog, knit across to last 2 sts, K2 tog: 22 sts.

Rows 9-19: Repeat Rows 7 and 8, 5 times; then repeat Row 7 once **more**: 12 sts.

All Sizes

Decrease Row: K5, K2 tog, K5: 11 sts.

BAND

Rows 1-7: Knit across.

Bind off all sts in **knit**, leave last st on needle; do **not** cut yarn.

Leg Bands

LEFT

With remaining st on larger size needles and with **right** side facing, pick up {37-43}{49-53-55} sts along Left leg opening *(Figs. 11a & b, page 61)*: {38-44}{50-54-56} sts.

Rows 1 and 2: Knit across.

Bind off all sts in **knit**.

RIGHT

With **right** side facing and using larger size needles, pick up {38-44}{50-54-56} sts along Right leg opening.

Rows 1 and 2: Knit across.

Bind off all sts in **knit**.

Sleeve

With **right** side facing and using larger size needles, pick up {3-3}{5-5-5} sts across cast on edge at underarm, knit across all sts of sleeve, removing scrap yarn and distributing sts evenly on needles to work in the round: {29-29}{33-35-37} sts.

Rnd 1: Knit around.

Repeat Rnd 1 once for Short Sleeve **or** until Sleeve measures approximately {5-5½}{6-6½-7}"/ {12.5-14}{15-16.5-18} cm from underarm for Long Sleeve.

RIBBING

Change to smaller size needles.

Row 1: K1, (P1, K1) around to last 2 sts, P2 tog: {28-28}{32-34-36} sts.

Rows 2 and 3: (K1, P1) around.

Bind off all sts **loosely** in ribbing.

Repeat for second sleeve.

Sew buttons to Front Flap, corresponding to buttonholes on Back Flap.

TASSELED HAT

Ribbing

With smaller size needles, cast on {64-68}{74-76-78} sts.

Slip one-fourth of the sts onto **each** of 4 smaller size double-pointed needles; place a split-ring marker to indicate the beginning of the round.

Rnds 1-8: (K1, P1) around.

Body

Change to larger needles.

Knit every round until Hat measures approximately {5½-6}{6½-7-7½}"/ {14-15}{16.5-18-19} cm from cast on edge.

Graft sts at top of hat *(Figs. 12a & b, page 62)*, OR bind off all sts in **knit** and sew seam.

Tassel

Make 2 Tassels as follows:

Cut a piece of cardboard 3" (7.5 cm) wide and 5" (12.5 cm) long. Wind a double strand of yarn lengthwise around the cardboard approximately 16 times. Cut an 18" (45.5 cm) length of yarn and insert it under all the strands at the top of the cardboard; pull up **tightly** and tie securely. Leave the yarn ends long enough to attach the tassel. Cut the yarn at the opposite end of the cardboard and then remove it *(Fig. A)*. Cut a 6" (15 cm) length of yarn and wrap it **tightly** around the tassel twice, ¾" (19 mm) below the top *(Fig. B)*; tie securely. Trim the ends.

Sew one tassel to each corner of hat.

Fig. A

Fig. B

GENERAL INSTRUCTIONS

ABBREVIATIONS

C6B	cable 6 back
cm	centimeters
K	knit
kfb	knit front and back
LT	left twist
mm	millimeters
P	purl
P2SSO	pass 2 slipped stitches over
Rnd(s)	Round(s)
RS	right side
RT	right twist
SSK	slip, slip, knit
st(s)	stitch(es)
tog	together
WS	wrong side
YO	yarn over

SYMBOLS & TERMS

★ — work instructions following ★ as many **more** times as indicated in addition to the first time.

( ) or [ ] — work enclosed instructions **as many** times as specified by the number immediately following **or** work all enclosed instructions in the stitch indicated **or** contains explanatory remarks.

colon (:) — the number(s) given after a colon at the end of a round or row denote(s) the number of stitches you should have on that round or row.

GAUGE

Exact gauge is **essential** for proper fit. Before beginning your project, make a sample swatch in the yarn and needle specified in the individual instructions. After completing the swatch, measure it, counting your stitches and rows or rounds carefully. If your swatch is larger or smaller than specified, **make another, changing needle size to get the correct gauge**. Keep trying until you find the size needle(s) that will give you the specified gauge.

KNIT TERMINOLOGY	
UNITED STATES	INTERNATIONAL
gauge =	tension
bind off =	cast off
yarn over (YO) =	yarn forward (yfwd) **or** yarn around needle (yrn)

Yarn Weight Symbol & Names	LACE 0	SUPER FINE 1	FINE 2	LIGHT 3	MEDIUM 4	BULKY 5	SUPER BULKY 6	JUMBO 7
Type of Yarns in Category	Fingering, size 10 crochet thread	Sock, Fingering, Baby	Sport, Baby	DK, Light Worsted	Worsted, Afghan, Aran	Chunky, Craft, Rug	Super Bulky, Roving	Jumbo, Roving
Knit Gauge Ranges in Stockinette St to 4" (10 cm)	33-40 sts**	27-32 sts	23-26 sts	21-24 sts	16-20 sts	12-15 sts	7-11 sts	6 sts and fewer
Advised Needle Size Range	000 to 1	1 to 3	3 to 5	5 to 7	7 to 9	9 to 11	11 to 17	17 and larger

* GUIDELINES ONLY: The chart above reflects the most commonly used gauges and needle sizes for specific yarn categories.

** Lace weight yarns are usually knitted on larger needles to create lacy openwork patterns. Accordingly, a gauge range is difficult to determine. Always follow the gauge stated in your pattern.

MARKERS

As a convenience to you, we have used markers to mark the beginning of a round. Place a marker as instructed. You may use a purchased marker or tie a length of contrasting color yarn around the needle. When you reach a marker on each round, slip it from the left needle to the right needle; remove it when no longer needed.

When using double-pointed needles, a split-ring marker can be placed around the first stitch in the round to indicated the beginning of the round. Move it up as the first stitch of each round is worked.

DOUBLE-POINTED NEEDLES

When working too few stitches to use a circular needle, double-pointed needles are required. Divide the stitches into fourths and slip one-fourth of the stitches onto each of 4 double-pointed needles, forming a square *(Fig. 1)*. With the fifth needle, work across the stitches on the first needle. You will now have an empty needle with which to work the stitches from the next needle. Work the first stitch of each needle firmly to prevent gaps.

Fig. 1

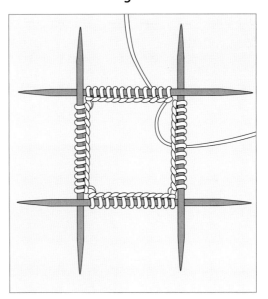

●○○○ BASIC	Projects using basic stitches. May include basic increases and decreases.
●●○○ EASY	Projects may include simple stitch patterns, color work, and/or shaping.
●●●○ INTERMEDIATE	Projects may include involved stitch patterns, color work, and/or shaping.
●●●● COMPLEX	Projects may include complex stitch patterns, color work, and/or shaping using a variety of techniques and stitches simultaneously.

KNITTING NEEDLES															
U.S.	0	1	2	3	4	5	6	7	8	9	10	10½	11	13	15	17
U.K.	13	12	11	10	9	8	7	6	5	4	3	2	1	00	000	---
Metric - mm	2	2.25	2.75	3.25	3.5	3.75	4	4.5	5	5.5	6	6.5	8	9	10	12.75

ZEROS

To consolidate the length of an involved pattern, zeros are sometimes used so that all sizes can be combined. For example, knit {0-1}{2-3-4} sts, means the first size would do nothing, the second size would K1, the third size would K2, the fourth size would K3, and the fifth size would K4.

E-WRAP CAST ON

Make a backward loop with the working yarn and place it on the right hand needle *(Fig. 2)*.

Fig. 2

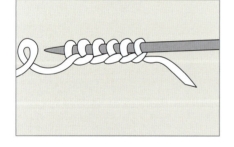

INCREASES

Yarn Over *(abbreviated YO)*
After a knit stitch, before a knit stitch
Bring the yarn forward **between** the needles, then back **over** the top of the right-hand needle, so that it is now in position to knit the next stitch *(Fig. 3a)*.

After a knit stitch, before a purl stitch
Bring the yarn forward **between** the needles, then back **over** the top of the right-hand needle and forward **between** the needles again, so that it is now in position to purl the next stitch *(Fig. 3b)*.

Fig. 3a

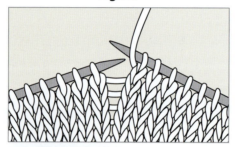

Fig. 3b

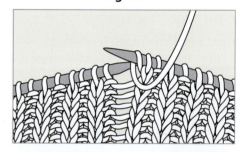

DECREASES

After a purl stitch, before a knit stitch

Take the yarn **over** the right-hand needle to the back, so that it is now in position to knit the next stitch *(Fig. 3c)*.

Fig. 3c

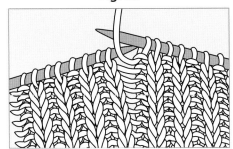

Knit 2 Together
(abbreviated K2 tog)

Insert the right needle into the **front** of the first two stitches on the left needle as if to **knit** *(Fig. 5)*, then **knit** them together as if they were one stitch.

Fig. 5

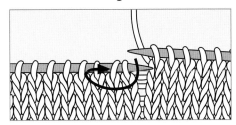

Slip, Slip, Knit *(abbreviated SSK)*

With yarn in **back** of work, separately slip two stitches as if to **knit** *(Fig. 7a)*. Insert the left needle into the **front** of both slipped stitches *(Fig. 7b)* and **knit** them together as if they were one stitch *(Fig. 7c)*.

Fig. 7a

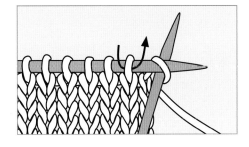

Knit in Front & Back
(abbreviated kfb)

Knit the next stitch but do **not** slip the old stitch off the left needle *(Fig. 4a)*. Insert the right needle into the **back** loop of the **same** stitch and knit it *(Fig. 4b)*, then slip the old stitch off the left needle.

Purl 2 Together
(abbreviated P2 tog)

Insert the right needle into the **front** of the first two stitches on the left needle as if to **purl** *(Fig. 6)*, then **purl** them together as if they were one stitch.

Fig. 7b

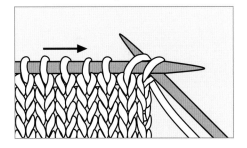

Fig. 6

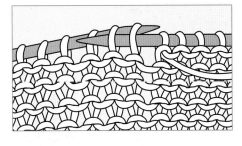

Fig. 4a

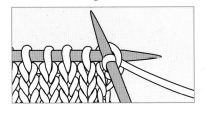

Fig. 4b

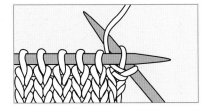

Fig. 7c

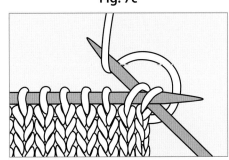

Knit 3 Together

(abbreviated K3 tog)

Insert the right needle into the **front** of the first three stitches on the left needle as if to **knit** *(Fig. 8)*, then **knit** them together as if they were one stitch.

Fig. 8

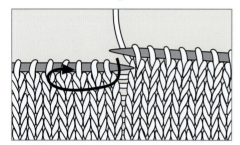

Slip 2 Together, Knit 1, Pass 2 Slipped Stitches Over

(abbreviated slip 2 tog, K1, P2SSO)

Slip two stitches together as if to **knit** *(Fig. 9a)*, then knit the next stitch. With the left needle, bring both slipped stitches over the knit stitch *(Fig. 9b)* and off the needle.

Fig. 9a

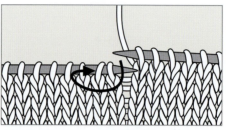

Fig. 9b

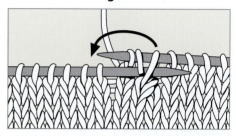

SHORT ROWS

Short rows are formed by working across some of the stitches before stopping and working back. In order to prevent holes, it is necessary to wrap the yarn around an unworked stitch before changing directions.

Wrapping Stitches

On a **right** side row, slip the next stitch as if to **purl**, bring the yarn forward *(Fig. 10a)*, slip the stitch back onto the left needle; turn the work.

On a **wrong** side row, slip the next stitch as if to **purl**, bring the yarn to the back *(Fig. 10b)*, slip the stitch back onto the left needle; turn the work.

Always knit or purl the wrap and the stitch it wraps together when you come to it *(Fig. 10c & d)*.

Fig. 10c

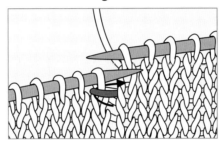

Fig. 10a

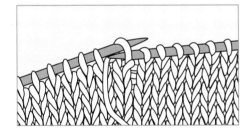

Fig. 10b

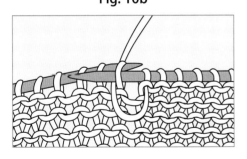

Fig. 10d

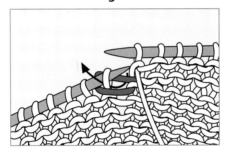

PICKING UP STITCHES

When instructed to pick up stitches, insert the needle from the **front** to the **back** under two strands at the edge of the worked piece *(Figs. 11a & b)*. Put the yarn around the needle as if to **knit**, then bring the needle with the yarn back through the stitch to the right side, resulting in a stitch on the needle.

Fig. 11a

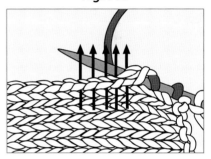

Fig. 11b

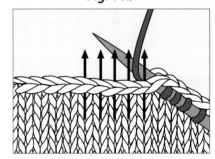

GRAFTING

Stitches to be woven are held on two knitting needles, with one behind the other and **wrong** sides together. Threaded yarn needle should be on the right edge of work. Work in the following sequence, pulling yarn through as if to **knit** or as if to **purl** with even tension and **keeping yarn under points of needles** to avoid tangling and extra loops.

Step 1: Purl the first stitch on the **front** needle, leave st on the needle *(Fig. 12a)*.

Step 2: Knit the first stitch on the **back** needle, leave st on the needle *(Fig. 12b)*.

Step 3: Knit the first stitch on the **front** needle, slip st off the needle.

Step 4: Purl the next stitch on the **front** needle, leave st on the needle.

Step 5: Purl the first stitch on the **back** needle, slip st off the needle.

Step 6: Knit the next stitch on the **back** needle, leave st on the needle.

Repeat Steps 3-6 across until all stitches are worked off the needles.

Fig. 12a

Fig. 12b

YARN INFORMATION

The projects in this book were made using Medium Weight Yarn. Any brand of medium weight yarn may be used. It is best to refer to the yardage/meters when determining how many balls or skeins to purchase. Remember, to arrive at the finished size, it is the GAUGE/TENSION that is important, not the brand of yarn.

For your convenience, listed below are the specific yarns used to create our photography models. Because yarn manufacturers make frequent changes in their product lines, you may sometimes find it necessary to use a substitute yarn or to search for the discontinued product at alternate suppliers (locally or online).

ALL OF A TWIST
Red Heart® Soft®
#9770 Rose Blush

B-A-B-Y LOVE
Premier® Anti-Pilling Everyday® Worsted
#100-47 Twilight Blue

DIAMOND BROCADE
Caron® Simply Soft® Tweeds™
#23002 Gray Heather Tweed

FRAMED CABLE
Caron® Simply Soft® Heathers™
#9503 Woodland Heather

LACE ACCENT
Premier® Anti-Pilling Everyday® Worsted
#100-10 Aubergine

MIXED BERRY
Premier® Anti-Pilling Everyday® Worsted
#200-22 Lilac Ridge

We have made every effort to ensure that these instructions are accurate and complete. We cannot, however be responsible for human error, typographical mistakes, or variations in individual work.

Production Team: Instructional/Technical Editor - Linda A. Daley; Senior Graphic Artist - Lora Puls; Photo Stylist - Lori Wenger; and Photographer - Jason Masters.

Copyright © 2019 by Leisure Arts, Inc., 104 Champs Blvd., STE 100, Maumelle, AR 72113-6738, www.leisurearts.com. All rights reserved. This publication is protected under federal copyright laws. Reproduction or distribution of this publication or any other Leisure Arts publication, including publications which are out of print, is prohibited unless specifically authorized. This includes, but is not limited to, any form of reproduction or distribution on or through the Internet, including posting, scanning, or e-mail transmission.

Made in U.S.A.